ALIAS AKBAR DEL PIOMBO

ALIAS AKBAR DEL PIOMBO:

Annotations to the Life and Work of Norman Rubington

GREGORY STEPHENSON

Ober-Limbo Verlag

Published by Ober-Limbo Verlag
Heidelberg, Germany

ISBN 978-87-971569-9-5

Cover illustration by Norman Rubington:
Untitled, 1989, courtesy of Norman Rubington.

Cover design & layout by
Birgit Stephenson

For Birgit

m'amie prodigieuse

Akbar del Piombo:
Pseudonym of Norman Rubington
(June 20, 1921 – January 1, 1991)

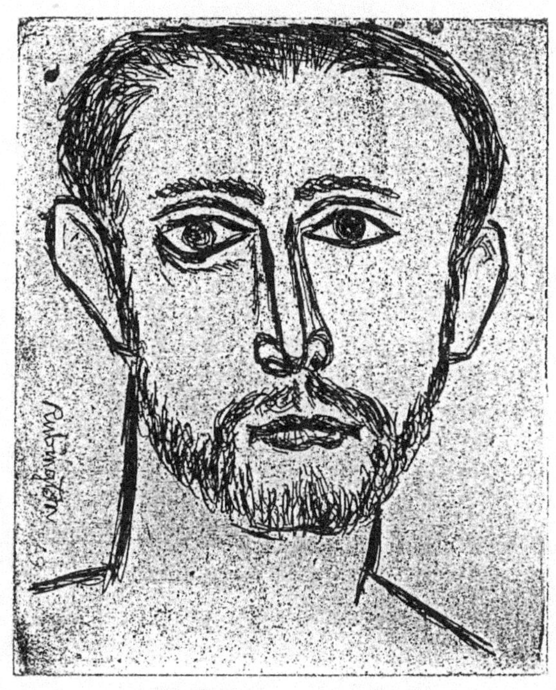

Unless otherwise attributed, all quotations from Norman Rubington appearing in the following are drawn from his letters to the author of these annotations. We corresponded from 1988 through 1990.
Self-portrait (above) by Norman Rubington, courtesy of Ann May Greene. Photographs by Frank Monaco and by unknown photographer, courtesy of Earl Rubington.

TRIBAL AFFILIATION

In response to a question I had posed to him in a letter concerning his acquaintance with the famous radio dramas of the 1930s, Norman Rubington wrote in reply that his favorite among them had been one – at present little known – called "The Lone Wolf Tribe." Norman recalled that – as required by the show's commercial sponsor – he had saved and submitted box tops of some product in order to receive in the mail what was, as he wrote: "a handsome sterling silver arrowhead to be worn as a pin." The silver pin was accompanied by a document imparting the tribe's principles and secret code. "I felt great," he remembered, "being an honorary member of this tribe. It must not have been very popular, which doesn't surprise me if I joined it, because I never met anyone else sporting that pin." (Letter to the author, June 26, 1989.)

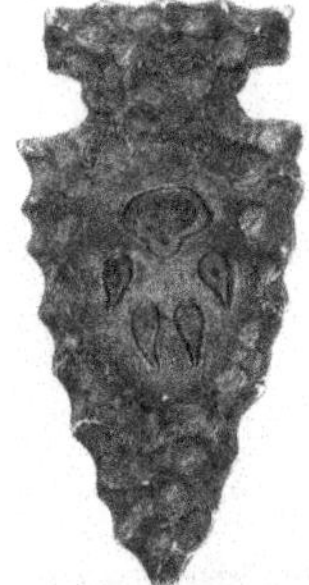

Lone Wolf
Tribe
arrowhead pin

The short-lived juvenile adventure series, "The Lone Wolf Tribe," sponsored by Wrigley's Gum, was broadcast three times a week from 1932 to 1933. Norman Rubington would thus have been 11 and 12 years old at the time of his fascination with the tribe, its ethos, emblems and practices.

CHINA

Having completed his studies at the Yale School of Fine Arts, in February of 1943, twenty-two year old Norman Rubington

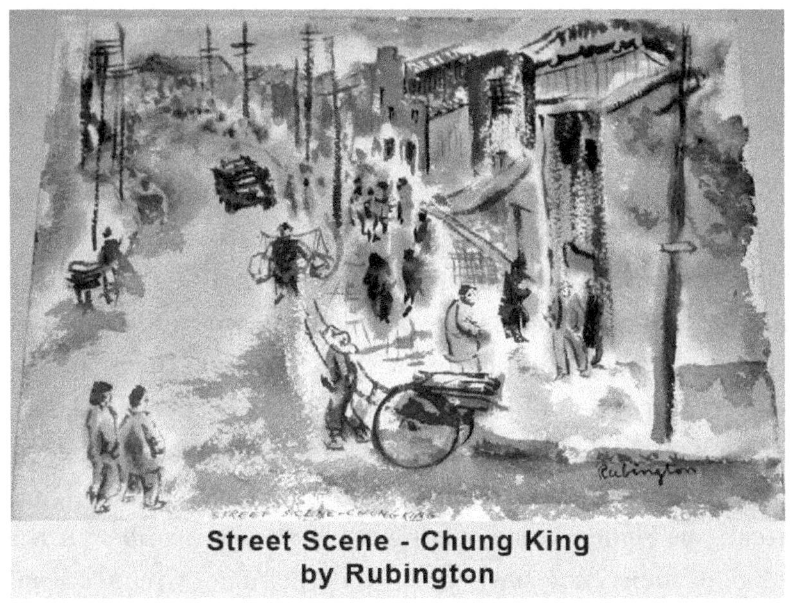

**Street Scene - Chung King
by Rubington**

was drafted into the U.S. Army, trained in map-making and the interpretation of aerial photographs, and stationed in China, then an area of U.S. military operations known as the CBI or China Burma India Theater.

"My wartime experience," Norman wrote to me, "amounted to a trip around the world. I was at no front and the closest I came to grips with action was a bullet zinging by my ear from a nervous Chinese sentry. We were on our way at midnight to the airfield to get fried eggs, a group on the night shift crossing a bridge when it happened. I was then with a mapping squadron and we were on a rush job preparing maps. ... There were only a few thousand Americans there [China] mainly at several airfields and the headquarters at Chungking. I was transferred to G-2 [i.e. military intelligence] because I had been to art school. So I flew up from Kunming leaving the old Flying Tigers barracks to find myself at a drafting table a few feet away from the top brass." (Letter to the author, November 14, 1988.)

During his tour of duty in China, Norman continued to paint and sketch, and contributed an illustration to the *China Worker's Daily* newspaper for September 27, 1943. Rubington's woodcut, portraying a mother and child, accompanies a poem titled "Lullaby," in which an impov-erished young mother pleads with the elements – the wind and the rain – not to disturb the sleep of her unfortunate child whose father is unem-ployed and for whom there is little to eat. (Newspaper sent as en-closure in letter to the author, October 4, 1988. A translation of the poem was made for me by Ms. Yuyu Li.)

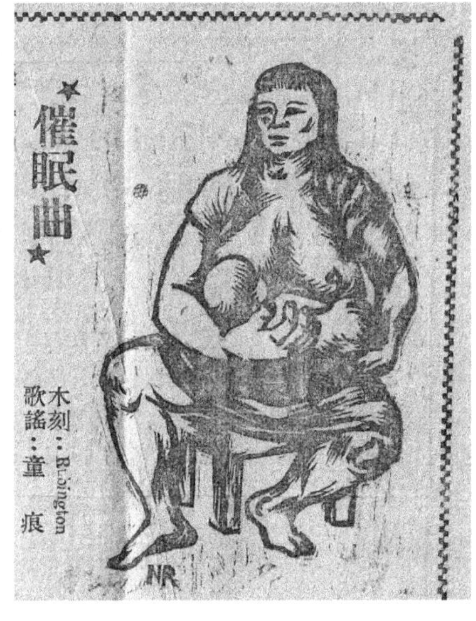

The bleakest memory of his time in China, Rubington wrote, was that of learning of the death of President Franklin Delano Roosevelt, a benign and revered figure of Norman's childhood, youth and young manhood. "We thought he would live forever," he related, and "no matter how dramatic and how deep the sorrow when Kennedy was assassinated I was never more shaken than when I heard that FDR had died. The circumstances alone are vivid. A barracks room in a colonial style house in the middle of Chungking, occupied by men of the Signal Corps and yours truly. I was fast asleep and yet at 2 in the morning woke up suddenly because the signal corps guys were talking. But softly. It was the tone of their voices not the volume that woke. A tone I'd never heard in this wisecracking bunch. Whispers. I heard no name but immediately knew who it was who had died. An amputee knows personal loss and this is as close as one can come to that without a doubt." (Letter to the author, June 26, 1989.)

Norman also recalled a far more pleasant occasion: "I had dinner one evening at the house of Mme. Sun Yat-sen whom I got to know in Chungking. She spoke of Paris and was undoubtedly the most sophisticated and down to earth person. I recall a lieutenant saying about her in the garden "She's the only person I ever met who could chew gum with dignity." (Letter to the author, December 7, 1988.)

Later in life, as Norman recounted, he refrained from telling people that he had been to China, having become "fed up with their blank looks of disbelief." (Letter to the author, November 14, 1988.)

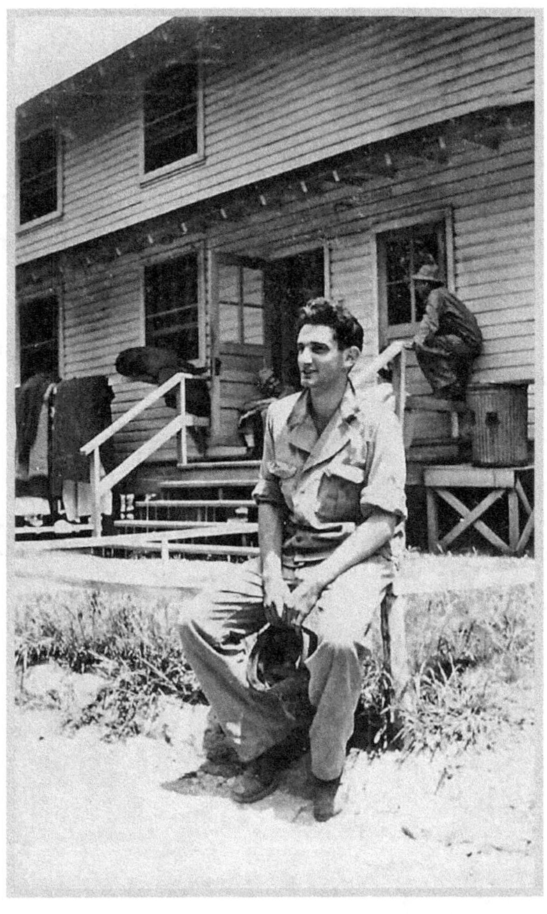

Left: Norman Rubington at Fort Belvoir, Virginia, June 1943, wearing khaki summer service uniform, holding helmet. Photographer unknown.

Norman recalled that among his fellow soldiers he had "the reputation of a naiveté my friends took advantage of. Nothing serious. They enjoyed telling me all kinds of stories because I believed every word and even now I don't even have the sense to blush at the admission." (Letter to the author, November 14, 1988.)

Right: Norman
Rubington at
Fort Belvoir,
Virginia, 1943,
in garrison cap
and olive drab
Class A uniform,
wearing rank of
Technical
Corporal.
Photographer
unknown.

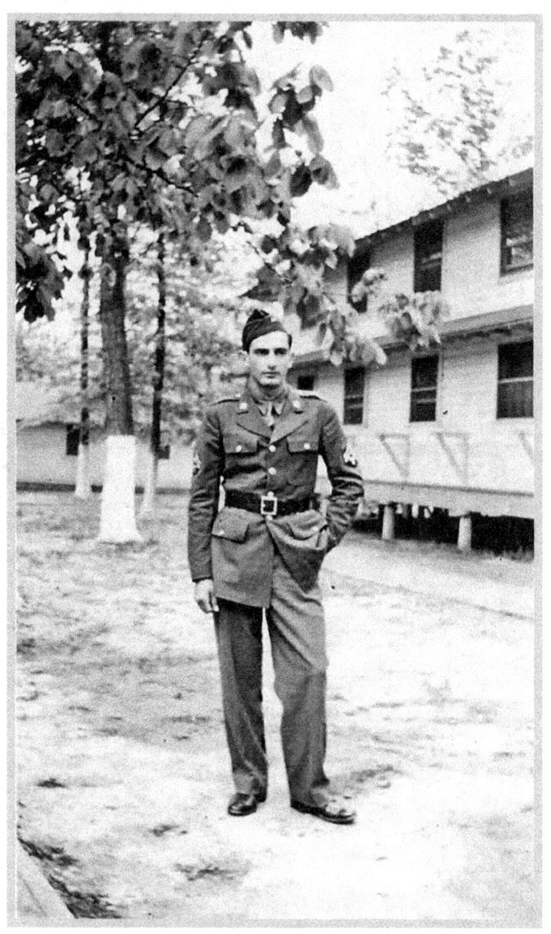

PARIS

Moving to Paris in 1946, Norman was a trailblazer among what was later to become the post-war wave of American artists and writers taking up residence in that city. Supporting himself during his first years there with monthly benefit checks issued to him under the G.I. Bill, he enrolled in the École des Beaux-Arts, then later in the Académie de la Grande Chaumière. "The G.I. Bill paid 75 dollars a month which was OK for a single man," he recalled. "Beer I think cost about two cents." (Letter to the author, March 6, 1990.)

"Instead of grabbing hold of the ladder here in the U.S. I went off to Europe," Norman wrote to me. But not without some foreboding and apprehension: "The Irish landlady of the walk-up I lived in for a while on 14th St. was thunderstruck when I told her I was leaving for the old country. This imposing woman who almost frightened me the way she tried to bring me back to my senses with her image of the decay and rot I was headed for. I was going backward while the world was moving on ... etc. etc. Why I didn't see it that way is something of a mystery, perhaps a matter of secret affinities, mysterious connections only barely felt. I am not even sure to what extent I was shying away from the competitiveness in America. There was a dream I had during the period. I was stuffing a steamer trunk with new clothing and making preparations for leaving and it bothered me for months. Only after I arrived in Paris did I see it as a warning against leaving. The troubling part of that dream was an accident in downtown New Haven when a truck drove into a trolley car. Suddenly French gendarmes were rushing to the scene. Perplexed, I followed after and the truck was hung with a banner reading *Lurcat Error*. (Lurcat was the name of a French painter.) Why his name was connected with error baffled me. The trolley was something I have always loved ever since my first ride. So this truck was well, you can figure that out. I had primitive-type solutions for the banner's message, like "lurking terror," or "look at error." That dream is still vivid even today. Then I started out against good sense, n'est-ce pas? But there were rewards amongst the miseries and whatever setbacks, no regrets." (Letter to the author, November 1, 1989.)

"I fell in love with the city instantly," Norman recounted, "a love affair that lasted almost twenty years. I have never felt so close to a landscape anywhere like the attachment I had for that city. Whatever happened good or bad was always right. Exactly like in a fine movie. It does often seem like a movie looking back on it." (Letter to the author, December 7, 1988.)

"Paris had the feeling of being the center of the world," he wrote in a subsequent letter, "I remember one day sitting at the Flore or the Deux Magots and thinking if you sat there long enough everyone would sooner or later pass by. ... During the Eisenhower years I often heard Americans complaining about the dullness in the states. In Paris there were cine clubs that showed experimental films, guys with energetic philosophies, theories, notions that made you feel the place was a hive of activity. Early on I was taking a late night walk, something you could do any time, no matter what the hour, and passing by a lit basement window heard a typewriter going full blast. I don't know why I felt something special about that. One could imagine all sorts of things burgeoning as if that typewriter were capturing ideas in the wind. To a painter it was the ideal city. Not arty but natural. Like the boulevards with trees and benches, the Seine with fishermen and painters, lovers and tramps. Why the more I think of it the more it seems utopian, which of course it wasn't, but the mind will have its way in these matters. Still and all it was quasi-idyllic in comparison with later developments. The dust of the world before the war hadn't completely settled and the mortar for the world to come hadn't yet dried." (Letter to the author, March 2, 1989.)

In response to my having asked Norman where he lived during his long sojourn in Paris, he replied: "a number of left bank hotels, several ateliers, including a storefront. Areas include Montparnasse and Montmartre and a place on the outskirts a morsel of a suburb called Malakoff. ... The storefront was situated on Rue Galande diagonally across from the old church of St. Julien-le-Pauvre. That store was a gas. The plate glass window was frosted and with a street lamp across the street passersby were cast in silhouette like on a movie screen. In summer with the transom open one could lie abed and view a true happening film, lovers pressed against the glass, their intimacies clearly audible."

"The landlady was a neurotic Romanian anti-Semite who was also a hypochondriac. One time when I lunted to the top floor to pay the rent she complained of ailments I never heard of as though she thought I was the doctor. I suggested she try some Alka-Seltzer. She did so and the following day knocked on my door with a glowing face to lavish her thanks for the wonderful remedy." (Letter to the author, January 16, 1990.)

In his book *Left Bank, Right Bank: Paris and Parisians* (London: William Kimber, 1952) Joseph Barry describes a visit to another of Rubington's flats: "I found him in a room on the ground floor, directly behind a fish shop of Rue Henri Barbusse off Boulevard Saint-Michel. He had knocked out a wall, put in glass panes, a wood-burning stove, a box-bed, a dog, an easel, some canvases and had begun to work. There were no toilet facilities and he had to get all his water from the fish shop." (*Left Bank, Right Bank*, p. 71.)

Barry considered Rubington to be "perhaps the most talented of the younger American artists in Paris," and described a typical day in the life of the "tall and gaunt," young artist. Rubington rose customarily at about 8:30 a.m., Barry wrote, fetched water for washing and for coffee from the nearby fish shop, fried an egg over the open flame of an alcohol lamp, then visited the Académie de la Grande Chaumiere, in which he was enrolled. Rubington seldom remained there for long, Barry noted, finding it, so the young artist declared, "stifling" to the creative impulse. Rubington is further cited as having commented that: "painting from life inhibits my work." Following his visit to the Académie, Rubington then returned to his flat and in solitude painted for the remainder of the morning and into the late afternoon. Evenings would be spent with fellow artists and ex-G.I.s, in a cheap Parisian bistro, eating, drinking, talking. *(Left Bank, Right Bank, pp. 71-72.)*

I had asked Norman about the presence in post-war Paris of desperate G.I. deserters still on the run from the C.I.D. and the military police. "Oh yes," he replied, "there were deserters. I was taken for one. Also for a DP [i.e. Displaced Person] by the gendarmes. Wearing old army clothes was something not unique but indigenous to those on the move, refugees and the uprooted. ... There was an incident in a bar in Montmartre where I was waiting for an amiable *fille de joie* to return when an MP entered and checked the papers of some G.I.'s at a table. He was there for a good five minutes which I knew was abnormal so after he left I went over to those guys and asked what was going on. They said he wasn't interested in them, it was me he was asking about. I was wearing an officer's coat, no military markings and a month's old beard, no tie, etc. etc. Actually they themselves weren't sure about me. As it turned out, the prostitute wasn't either. The next morning we had an awful spat, she demanding to know who I really was and not believing anything I said. Not altogether surprising since my French was in a formative stage larded with thick American accent. .... Another time a friend and I were wandering the streets and I had just purchased a sausage which I kept in the breast pocket of my field jacket. We were stopped by two "Hirondelles" (the cops on bikes) and the one interrogating me patted me for secreted arms and feeling the sausage broke out in an exultant Aha! and grabbed the deadly instrument. I shall never forget the look on his face." (Letter to the author, March 16, 1990.)

In a letter dated September 1, 1988, Norman referred to his years in Paris as "the heroic period" of his life, by which he meant that it was at that time and in that fertile environment that his art flourished. While living in Paris he experimented with styles and techniques (including teaching himself the process of aquatint) and began to achieve a degree of recognition among art critics for his vision and proficiency in a variety of media. Already in 1948, his work was included in an exhibition at the Salon d'Automne, followed by a solo exhibit in 1950 at Galerie Huit (a gallery he helped to create together with other American artists resident in Paris, located at no. 8 rue Saint-Julien-le-Pauvre.) In 1951, he won the prestigious Prix de Rome.

It was also during this period that Rubington began to undertake what were at the outset, tentative, informal forays into the art of collage, scouring "the Flea Market and second-hand book stalls for rare material." (Letter to the author, August 31, 1988.) An intriguing, exhilarating, compelling aspect of composing surreal/satirical collages out of 19th century engravings was, Norman wrote, that "there would be moments, the occasional surprises that tease one along, the happenstance, the serendipity or whatever it may be ... ." (Letter to the author, August 5, 1988.) Indeed, at times he found that assembling collages could become obsessional. He would sit on the floor of his studio-flat, he recalled, surrounded by a sea of paper, oblivious to all else. "Making collages day after day all day long for days on end," Norman remembered, "caused a curious effect when I stepped outdoors. All the world was rendered in engraving lines."

(Letter to the author, December 10, 1990.) At first an amusing appendage to his art, collage making was to become for Rubington what would was, in effect, a distinct, autonomous artistic identity.

EROTICA

Few things, it would seem, concentrate the mind quite so effectively as does the imminent prospect of penury. Norman's eligibility for monthly checks under the terms of the G.I. Bill having expired, he found himself with scarcely a sou in his pocket. Dejected and on the verge of selling his last material resource – his scooter – he visited a sculptor friend of his from whom he might expect some sympathy. Norman was astonished to find his friend furiously engaged in typing a draft manuscript for the infamous Olympia Press, publishers of erotica. His friend (likewise impoverished and desperate) informed him that if Maurice Girodias, the editor of the Olympia Press, accepted the initial 30 page draft of an erotic novel, then an advance payment would be made to the author. Ultimately, the fee for writing a "dirty book" for Girodias would be the equivalent in French francs of 500 dollars, a fortune in post-war Paris.

Inspired by the possibility of earning such a large sum, Norman spent the following three days and nights typing a 30 page draft to submit to Girodias. To his considerable surprise, the draft was accepted and Norman drew his advance from Girodias's secretary. The completed novel (composed in three weeks) was titled *Who Pushed Paula?* and appeared under the pseudonym (chosen by Girodias) of Akbar del Piombo. Encouraged by Girodias to undertake further such licentious narratives, Norman produced three more in quick succession.

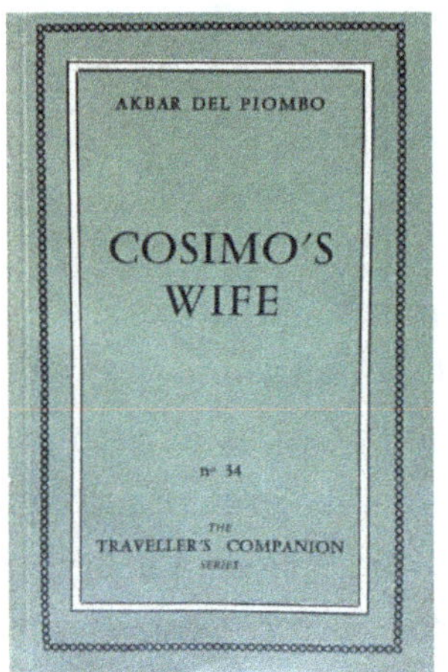

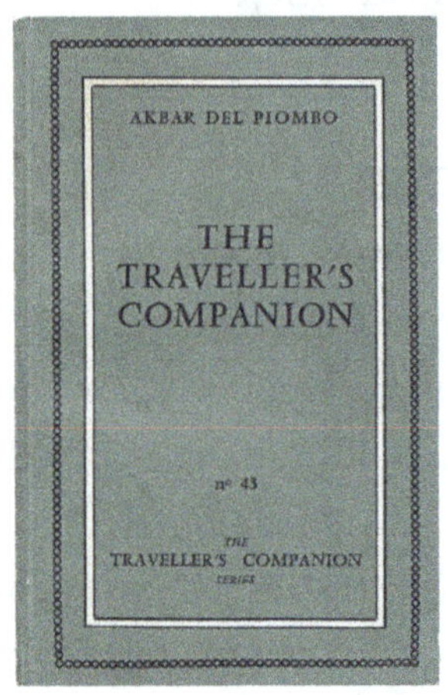

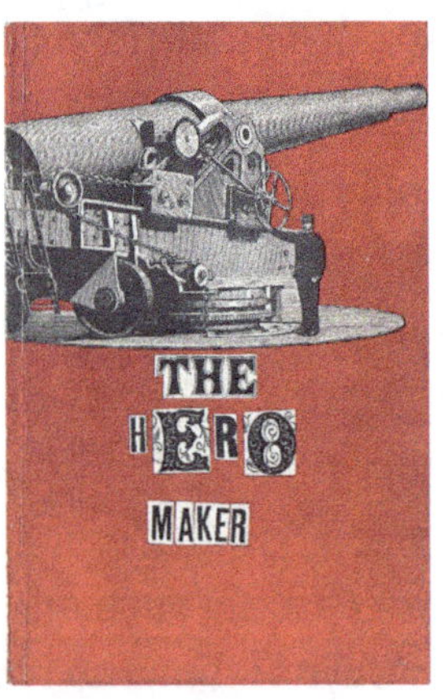

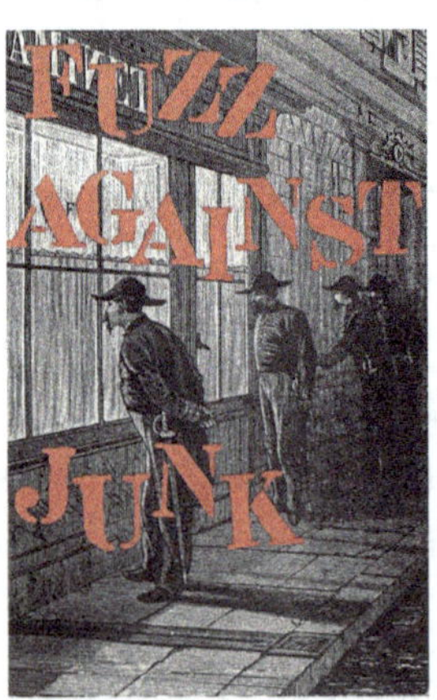

The Akbar del Piombo novels may be seen as a kind of pastiche of pornography. Indeed, the scenes of coupling in the novels are so baroque, so excessive, so fantastical as to constitute a kind of parody of the genre. In an article on the

Olympia Press in *Time* magazine ("Shy Pornographer," November 3, 1961, vol. lxxviii, no. 21) Norman asserted that "The books have so much filth that they're not filthy. They're zany, like the Marx Brothers." A similar assessment of the Akbar del Piombo novels is offered by John Calder in his memoir, *The Garden of Eros: The Story of the Post-War Expatriates & the Post-War Literary Scene* (Alma Books, London, 2014.) Of Rubington's salacious literary labors for the Olympia Press, Calder remarks: "The flights of imagination and descriptive extravagance that were written under the name Akbar del Piombo plumbed the carnal depths of humorous pornography." (p. 111.)

Writing as Akbar del Piombo, Norman Rubington's prose contributions to the disreputable/celebrated Traveller's Companion Series of the Olympia Press consist of the following volumes: *Who Pushed Paula?* no. 26 (Paris: 1956); *Skirts*, no. 27 (Paris: 1956); *Cosimo's Wife*, no. 34 (Paris: 1957); and *The Traveller's Companion*, no. 43 (Paris: 1957.) Three of these books (*Paula, Cosimo & Companion*) were later re-titled and collected as a trilogy in a volume titled *The Fetish Crowd*, no. 73, 1959, reprinted 1965. However hastily written, and however playfully jocular in spirit, the Akbar del Piombo novels seem still to enjoy perennial popularity among readers of the genre. All have been widely translated, reprinted and pirated, and all are currently available as e-books.

Additionally, the Olympia Press published four of Norman's satirical collage novels, with prose texts by Akbar del Piombo and illustrations by "Rubington." The first of these, *Fuzz Against Junk* (Paris: 1959) became an instant cult classic and was followed by *The Hero Maker* (Paris: 1960), *The Boiler Maker* (Paris: 1961) and *Is That You Simon?* (Paris: 1961.) For backgrounds to and acute thematic analysis of the collage novels, see "Mutinous Jester: Akbar del Piombo's Collage Novels" by Gregory Stephenson in the online journal *Empty Mirror:*https://www.emptymirrorbooks.com/literature/collage-novels-akbar-del-piombo. This article is also collected in *The Ragged Promised Land: Jack Kerouac's America & Other Scenes* by Gregory Stephenson, Ober-Limbo Verlag, 2020.

BLEECKER STREET

"Those last years in Paris were barren," Norman wrote to me in a letter dated November 1, 1989. In compliance, then, with the restless and mysterious imperatives of the spirit, in 1969, he returned to the United States, settling in New York City, in a flat at no. 13 Bleecker Street. Here amid the world's welter, in solitude, he continued vigorously to create: painting, sculpting, drawing, experimenting with film, writing poetry, and under his Akbar del Piombo nom-de-plume publishing two more collage novels: *Moonglow* (New York: Beach Books, 1969) and *Age of Ages: A Gothic Science Fiction Trip to the Apocalyse* (serialized in *Heavy Metal* from April 1977 to February 1978.) He published poems in little magazines, including *Pearl, Ins & Outs* and *Not Guity,* and contributed collages and humorous pieces to *National Lampoon, Rolling Stone, Other Scenes, High Times, S.NOB, International Times* and other avant-garde or counter-cultural periodicals whose readership was attuned to his hip, outré comedy.

"What a neigborhood," he wrote of Bleecker Street, "just a block or so down it is the pits, the remnant of the original skid row." (Letter to the author, 9 May 1989.) Contrasting his present location to my own descriptions of Copenhagen, he lamented the absence in his surroundings of any "pastoral elements," together with the ominous presence of an ugly, destructive psychic undercurrent manifested in the streets of NYC: "only a few blocks away on Broadway are angry posters and graffiti itching to tear the city down." (Letter to the author, 21 May 1990.)

Norman deplored what he saw as the merciless mercenary ethos of the city and its toll in human misery, writing that NYC was characterized by "a hard cynical ambiance, commercial glut and pollution. The street outside my window which once harbored strays from the Bowery, the groggy bums and winos, now has crackheads turning on in doorways, sneaking away from cops, wheeling and dealing, visions as limited as their vocabulary." (Letter to the author, March 2, 1989.) The sordidness and menace of the city seemed to him to culminate in an incident immediately outside his residence in August of 1989 when "a sniper fired into the street and Bleecker Street made the evening TV with police SWAT teams on the rooftops .... scarcely believable." (Letter to the author, August 23, 1989.)

The destructive undercurrent of the city even contrived to penetrate the very walls of his modest flat in the guise of intolerable noise inflicted upon him by a neighbor. At first Norman tried ear plugs, he wrote, but these proving insufficient: "I had a long and difficult battle with a neighbor, who played hard rock that blasted this tiny place. The different phases of that battle included pouring water to blow out his electrical system, procuring several Hi-Fi's and on one memorable night leaving them on full blast with Beethoven and Tchaikovsky and leaving the place to its hell." (Letter to the author, June 26, 1989.)

In his letters, Norman ruefully acknowledged that disorder was the order of the day both in his flat and in his mind. "The mental clutter looms as despairingly as the physical," he wrote, providing by way of evidence a brief description of the interior of his congested and bestrewn habitat: "There's hardly a corner visible with all that's clambering for space, a woebegone plant with a stalk as thin as a needle and only a drooping remnant of the tiny leaves that were meant to rise in some tropical forest. Another plant struggles bravely in a dark corner living by its wits on a careful consumption, limiting itself to water like sailors adrift. To catalogue all the rest would be as futile as it is bewildering." (Letter to the author, June 26, 1989.) I have a sense that the disorder – within and without – to which Norman alludes was likely both the fertile ground and the debris and leavings of his vibrant, insurgent imagination. A certain disarray would seem to have served to facilitate in his art and thinking the chance configurations in which he delighted, the fortuitous conjunctions, the unlikely con-currences and continuities, the element of creative adventure that he referred to as "the lure of the unexpected that at times turns up in connections that somehow tickle." (Letter to the author, May 21, 1990.)

PEN FOR HIRE

Was it lack of funds or was it, perhaps, the peculiar challenges and arcane satisfactions inherent in the tasks themselves that impelled Norman's ventures into genre writing? I did not ask him and he did not volunteer his motivation for the pseudonymous writing he took up after his return to the United States. I imagine, though, that his incentive in under-taking to write the unlikely works he produced during the late 1960s and 1970s was the never-ending hand-to-mouth hard-ship of an artist's life, though he may also have relished the incongruities – the sheer weirdness – implicit in turning his hand to such work.

In the late 1960s, Norman wrote another erotic novel for the Olympia Press which had recently relocated to New York City. Titled *The House in Lodz* and published as no. 462 in the Traveller's Companion Series (New York: Olympia Press, 1969) the novel is an hallucinated, darkly comic, fiercely

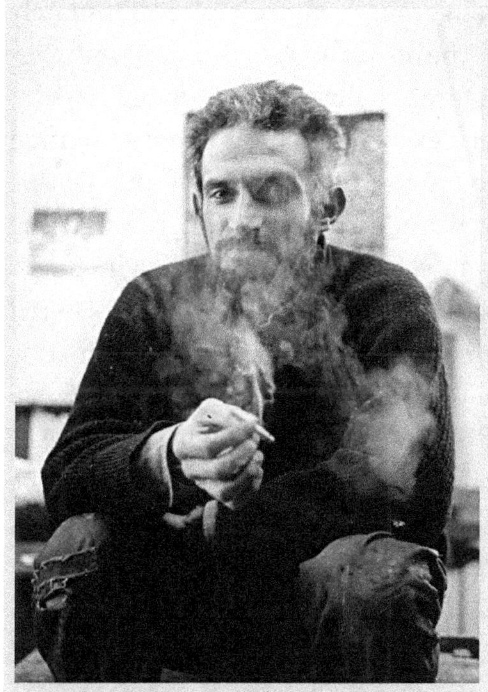

Photograph by Frank Monaco, courtesy of Earl Rubington

satirical story which includes reflections on the writing of pornography and the role of pornography in society. "Dirty it up," a publisher of porn tells a faltering, depleted, seasoned writer of erotica in the book, "or I can't sell it to my 42nd Street gang. The elite want meat. They don't need to hear about life's problems, they got enough as it is." The novel's figure of the disinclined, disenchanted pornographic author (a self-reflexive alter-ego of the author of *The House in Lodz*?) later ponders whether the appeal of raw, ruthless sex seemingly so popular among the readership of the "dirty books" he writes might not disclose a dark, elemental human truth concerning the dangerously unprincipled, ultimately ungovernable nature of the erotic impulse upon the ever tenuous control of which force civilization is founded.

Norman's further excursions into genre writing include at least two and perhaps all four of the Gothic Romance novels published under the pseudonym of "Leslie Paige." The Leslie Paige novels entered in copyright under Norman Rubington's name in the card catalog of the United States Copyright Office are: *A House Possessed*, published by Tower Publications, New York, 1974; and *She Walks in Shadow*, printed by the same publisher in the same year. ("Ellen longed for a tranquil life, but the fates seemed to be working against her.") It would appear that no copyright was registered for the other two Leslie Paige titles: *Queen of Hearts* and *Dying Embers*, both of which were published by Tower Publications in 1974. I suspect that they, too, were written by Norman, especially as the latter novel is said to be set in Rome and in Paris, both cities Norman knew well.

Under the house pseudonym of "John W. Hardin," Norman penned a western titled *The Comancheros,* printed by Nordon Publications, New York, 1973; and under another house pseudonym, "John Benteen," he wrote another western, *Bounty Killer,* Nordon Publications, New York, 1975. Both of these books are instalments in The Sundance Series (numbers 11 and 15, respectively) featuring a protagonist named Jim Sundance, the offspring of an English trader and a Cheyenne woman. Sundance is a "gun-for-hire" who nevertheless always fights on the side of the oppressed and the exploited. The cover of *The Comancheros* names the author of the novel as "Jack Slade," but the title page of the book designates the author as "John W. Hardin." According to the United States Copyright Office, the actual author of *The Comancheros* is Norman Rubington, in whose name the book is copyrighted.

In the catalog of the United States Copyright Office, Norman Rubington is also credited as the editor of three volumes in the genre of True Crime. These include: *The Short Dirty Life of a Mafia Killer* by George Damico, Belmont Tower Books, 1975 ("The authentic brutal story of a professional executioner;") *Street Hustler,* Leisure Books, New York, 1975 ("The whole sordid story of street hookers and their pimps;") and *Mugger* by "Spanish John," ("The life story of a street criminal – a vicious cunning thug – told in his own words") published by Belmont Tower Books in 1975.

Of Norman's contributions to the field of genre writing, I have read only two: *Mugger* and *The Comancheros.*

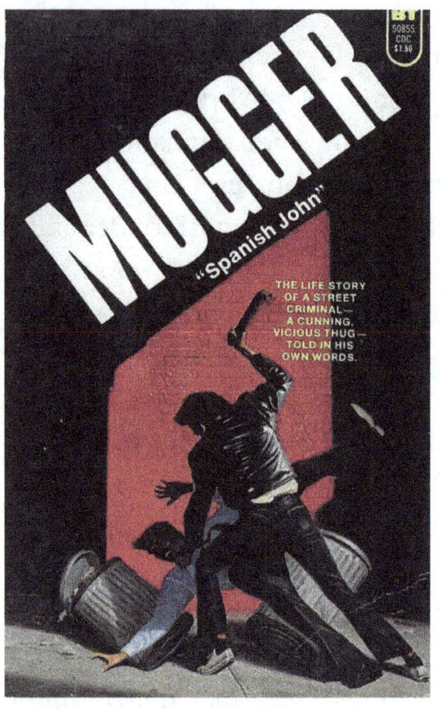

(Vintage paperbacks, as readers may be aware, have grown to be increasingly uncommon and can be expensive.) *Mugger* is of interest because (unlike the other books that Norman edited) the title page of the book states that the text is "Edited by Norman Rubington," and because the first person narrative by "Spanish John" is preceded by a seven page "Editor's Note" written by Rubington. In his note to the text, Rubington makes clear from the outset the abhorrent nature of the account that follows and of the man who recounts it. "Spanish John" is, Rubington states, "a merciless, conscience-less thief and murderer ... and the whole world will benefit when, someone, police or vigilante, finally kills him." Rubington then addresses the issue of why the publishers chose to print the book. "Some of our editors," he reports, "were against it from the moment they listened to the tape made by Spanish John." Ultimately, however, the editors concluded that the book which depicts in stark detail a brutal aspect of life in a modern metropolis might as such aid in illuminating the topic of urban street crime. Rubington then engages in a brief denunciation of the city of New York for providing a suitably rank and bounteous environment for persons such as "Spanish John." "New York," Rubington contends, "has its unique brand of *strangeness.* It is a wild city, a highly dangerous city," whose law-abiding inhabitants seem to him to be all too passive and acquiescent in their view of street crime, deeming it inevitable, irremediable, and in this way becoming unwitting accomplices in their own victimization. (A similarly dim view of New York City, it will be recalled, is expressed in Norman's letters.)

As for the narrator's transcribed oral version of his life and livelihood, it is plain that "Spanish John" is a self-savoring sociopath. He crows over his triumphs, vaunts his cunning and his material wealth, and insults and taunts his audience to whom he feels utterly superior. Repeatedly, in the course of his gloating narrative, he accuses his prospective readers of secretly envying his freedom from moral restraints and of taking vicarious pleasure in his violent exploits. And, alas, for certain uncritical readers – those seeking temporary relief from their monotonous lives in chronicles of true crime – that may, indeed, be the case. Sadly, the appeal of this book to such readers would seem to confirm what William James called our "aboriginal capacity for murderous excitement." (*Essays, Comments & Reviews,* ed. by Frederick Burkhard et al. Cambridge, MA, Harvard University Press, 1987, p. 171.)

It is as if "Spanish John" inadvertently reveals himself to be human only in the strictest biological sense of the term.

In effect, he is the spiritually vacant agent of some malign energy or power in the universe. Small wonder, then, that Rubington – allied to the creative forces of Beauty, Truth and Humor – feels for him such revulsion and wishes him dead.

In one of the more high-handed and half-baked pronouncements to which he was sometimes given, D.H. Lawrence declared that "The essential American soul is hard, isolate, stoic, and a killer." (*Studies in Classic American Literature,* N.Y. Viking, 1968, p. 62.) However manifestly misconceived this is as a generalization, I will concede that the description can be seen to be a fairly apt (if incomplete) characterization of the figure of Jim Sundance, the protagonist of The Sundance Series of western novels, and the central figure in Norman's novel, *The Comancheros.*

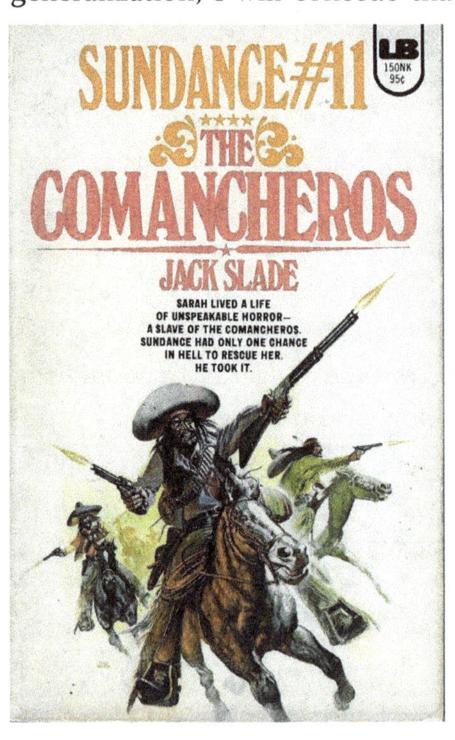

The novel is written with proper respect both for prospective readers and for the conventions of the adult western genre. These latter include: a valiant loner as protagonist, a truly vicious, villainous antagonist, an exotic western locale (in this case, mountains and deserts) and the motifs of revenge, pursuit, rescue, flight and righteous, regenerative violence. Rubington has clearly taken care to familiarize himself with details of the geography, geology, weather and plant life of the western United States (specifically the New Mexico territory) as well as acquainting himself with frontier firearms.

The story, briefly told, consists of Jim Sundance's efforts to avenge the torture-murder of his friends the MacIvers family at the hands of the depraved marauder Eldon Riggs and his barbarous, bloodthirsty outlaw band known as the Comancheros, and to rescue from captivity young Sarah MacIvers whom the bandits have abducted.

Jim Sundance is dissimilar to other loner heroes of the western in that he is a consummate outsider, a "half-breed," held in contempt both by Indians and by white settlers. (Even among the crème-de-la-scum of the Comancheros whose ranks he infiltrates: "They all wanted to see him dead because he was an outsider.") Apart from the unfavourable circumstance of his parentage, he possesses every heroic virtue and ability, including astute insight into the character and motivations of others.

By subtle touches, Rubington discloses unexpected, atypical traits of Jim Sundance's archetypal-heroic-chivalric psychological make-up. Readers learn that the hardened hero cannot bear the pain of others. Early in the novel, he shoots a cow to end its suffering, and in the course of the story shoots two men to end or prevent their torment. We also learn that despite his stoicism he is deeply dismayed by the corruption and suffering he witnesses. "The God damned world is so full of pain," he reflects, and reveals that he has on occasion sought oblivion in drink because "once in a while he couldn't stand one more speck of all the dirt that covered the world and the people who lived in it."

In common with numerous novels in the western genre, the main themes of *The Comancheros* are Good versus Evil, and Order versus Anarchy. A sub-theme pursued by the author is that of a somewhat bleak perspective on human nature. The villainous Eldon Riggs is described in terms of animal similes, and nearly all other figures in the novel (whether law-abiding settlers or outlaws) are depicted as driven by vanity, cowardice, lust, bloodlust and avariciousness. Characters are consistently delineated in terms of the foul odors they emanate: fetid breath, and the smells of urine, vomit, and stale sweat. Apart from Jim Sundance, the only other characters in the story who act out of integrity are the figure of the Catholic priest who refuses to violate the tenets of his faith, and Sarah MacIvers who matures in the course of her ordeal to the degree that in the end she can even compassionate Eldon Riggs, the man who murdered her parents.

An endearing Rubingtonian touch to this fast-paced, relentlessly harsh, western action-narrative occurs in the form of a passage which describes the hero's fondness for consuming marijuana, a supply of which he carries with him on his journey and smokes in a pipe. "Riding easily, he sucked the acrid smoke deep into his lungs," Rubington writes, "now all he felt was a sense of relaxing, the way some white men seemed to loosen up and take things easier after a few drinks of whiskey. But there was something else and he knew it didn't come with liquor: the morning colors that dappled the low brown hills he was riding through seemed deeper to his eyes, to his mind. It was as if he could take in the whole world more clearly." Hee hee. Yippee ki-yay! A weed-head hero of the Wild West! Ah, Norman.

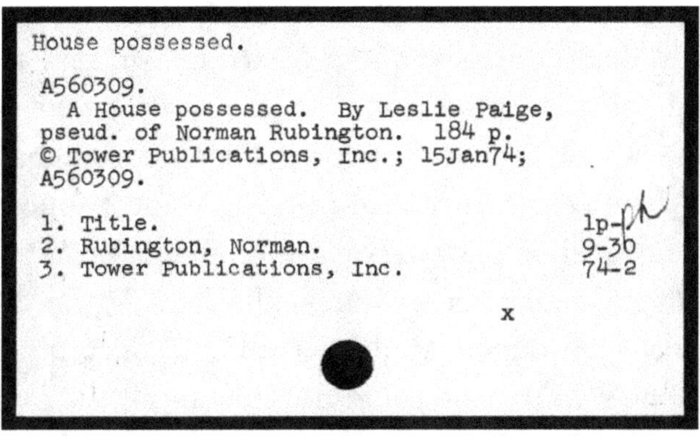

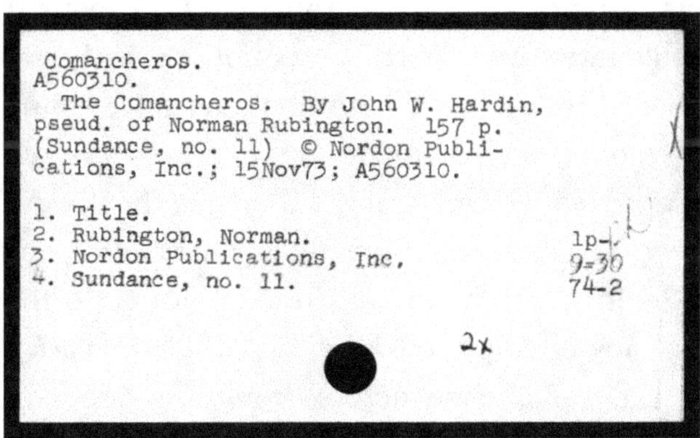

ANIMUS GIRODIAS

In June of 1965, the Olympia Press re-issued *The Fetish Crowd*, once again under the pseudonym of Akbar del Piombo. On a verso page facing the title page was printed: "Other works by William Burroughs published by the Olympia Press / *The Soft Machine* / *The Ticket That Exploded.*" What appears to have been a mistake made by the printer, Imprimerie Croutzet of Paris, who was in June of 1965 simultaneously engaged in reprinting William Burroughs' *The Naked Lunch*, gave rise to widespread speculation and, indeed, conviction, that Akbar del Piombo was a pseudonym for William Burroughs, and that all of the novels and collage-novels previously published by the Olympia Press under the nom-de-plume of Akbar del Piombo had been authored by Burroughs.

I once questioned Maurice Girodias concerning this matter and he said that he could not now recall the cause of the mix-up. He thought perhaps it was due to a misprint in an Olympia Press catalog. But Girodias was adamant that it was not deliberate on his part. It was not a ruse, he said, to increase sales of the Akbar del Piombo books. He would not, he said, have done such a thing, nor would the two authors have countenanced it. (Only later, did I make the discovery of the incorrect "Other works by William Burroughs" entry in the reprint edition of *The Fetish Crowd*. I note also that my copy of the 1965 Olympia Press reprint of *The Naked Lunch* carries on the verso page across from the title page no statement of "Other works by William Burroughs published by the Olympia Press." This would seem to indicate that the explanation that the Imprimerie Croutzet made a mistake in binding *The Fetish Crowd* may well be valid.)

Norman, however, was of another opinion. Despite (or perhaps because of) his long-standing association with Girodias, Norman considered his publisher to be of a scheming and deceitful character. "About that Burroughs mix-up," Norman wrote, "I knew very well about that insert in *The Fetish Crowd.* I happened to have been there when the book came out and when I saw that insert I hit the ceiling. He just sat there with that unspeakable and indefinable Gallic trait, the cat that ate the canary sneer. ... He said it was a printer's error. Horse manure. Having discovered a genius author whom he didn't recognize at first he now figures he'll exploit the name. Piombo won't ever sell as fast. Knowing nom-de-plumes cover a world of sin who would be the wiser? He did a similar operation some time later when his brother [i.e. Eric Kahane] translated a couple of my picture books into French. At the back of the book Girodias inserted a plug for his nightclub, saying if you enjoyed the ambiance of this literature you will find the same at his establishment. Chutzpah is his middle name. So we had a falling out over that nastiness and that put a crimp in the American appearance of *Fuzz* [printed by the Citadel Press, New York, 1961, "A Far-Out Book."] so that when it was finally available in bookstores, the fine review it got was totally forgotten." (Letter to the author, October 6, 1990.)

In May of 1990, the second volume of Maurice Girodias' memoirs – *Une Journée sur la Terre: Les Jardins d'Éros* – appeared in France. Soon after the publication of the book, in early July of the same year, Girodias died suddenly during the course of a radio interview. I ordered and read the memoirs and was dismayed to see the scornfully abusive description of Norman Rubington that Girodias had penned. It amounted to nothing less than character assassination. The two men had, after all, known and worked with each other for nearly four decades.

Girodias records in *Une Journée* that he first encountered Norman at Gaït Frogé's English Bookshop on the rue de Seine. Girodias begins his defamatory characterization of Rubington by pronouncing him "a sexual predator." He then goes on to write:

"Provocative, inventive and shameless, with biting wit Norman would assault the most vulnerable of victims; at the same time, beneath his boasting and his lack of restraint, he hid a romantic soul. His cartoonish cruelty made all the little goslings squeal with delight at his gloomy moods... This legendary personage had installed himself in the intimate sphere of Gaït [Frogé] and he thrived there.

"A genuine and quintessential New Yorker, he was without a doubt the first offspring of that city of dreams who was to me the very incarnation of my own image of it. A tough guy, a hard guy, who might have been the head of a gang... He had a great sense of humor and the soul of an artist; these served to pull him in opposite directions: in painting he could have made a career for himself despite possessing in excess both ability and an inclination to distraction; or he might have pursued a career in writing for which he was very gifted... His problem was that "work" and "success" seemed to him intolerable because they represented concessions made to a corrupt and corrupting bourgeois society... Instead, he preferred living off women – no matter the cost.

"Norman was known in all of the Anglophone circles of Paris as the oldest beneficiary of [the G.I. Bill.] He was, in that regard, a champion of a Methuselah-like duration. Yet this had not prevented him from seducing and marrying a pleasant pharmacist from the 11th arrondissement in order to secure for himself a cosy nook by the fire while winter winds were blowing; but it was in the 6th arrondissement that Rubington, then known as "The Rube", practiced his insolent seductions.

"His chiselled features gave him a sulphurous charm that caused café waitresses to swoon – and he was by no means averse to their attentiveness to him; nor did he scorn bourgeois women of luxurious habits and opulent bodies, to whom he was pleased to offer himself. Indeed, why not? They all measured him and studied him at a distance. He had but to choose among them, but he took his time because he liked being in demand." (Excerpt from Maurice Girodias: *Une Journée sur la terre, II, Les jardins d'Éros*, Éditions de la Difference, Paris 1990, pp. 260-261. Translation from the French by Birgit Stephenson.)

I photocopied the two pages of the book on which the offensive characterization of Norman was printed and sent them to him as an enclosure in my next letter. His fiery reply was printed in all capital letters.

"RUBE!!! HE DID TWO WHOLE PAGES, GREGORY, TWO ENTIRE PAGES THE MOST ANYONE HAD EVER PUT IN PRINT ON ME

AND THROUGH EVERY SENTENCE OF HIS IMAGINATIVE PROSE I COULD HEAR THE CHUCKLES IN THE BACKGROUND. MAURICE WAS WRITING THAT FOR *ME*. ENJOYING EVERY WRITHING (AS HE HOPED) KNEE-JERK RESPONSE TO THIS GENTEEL CALUMNY. A PIECE OF FICTIONAL EXPERIMENTATION FOR THE NOVEL HE NEVER WROTE BUT THE JOY OF AMPLIFICATION AND THE DEGREE OF FINESSE TO A WELL-TURNED THRUST HE WAS POSITIVE WOULD HAVE ME DROOLING TO PARRY AND COUNTERATTACK. I NOTE NOT A WORD ON THE SPECIES OF NOVELS THAT I DID FOR THAT HOUSE, JUST A BRIEF NOTE OF HAVING SOME TALENT THATAWAY. OH HE IS HAVING FUN RIGHT NOW BREATHING OVER MY SHOULDER IF SPIRITS BREATHE AND GURGLING AT EVERY BOUNCE AND SLIP OF THE TYPEWRITER POUNDING AWAY UNDER HIS INSPIRATION, SECURE FROM ATTACK AND RELISHING THE BRILLIANCE IN A WAY ONLY A SPIRIT CAN. AFTER ALL, A LAUGH IN LIFE SOON DIES DOWN. A JOKE IS DIMINISHED WHEN DONE, GOES STALE WITH TIME. BUT WHERE HE GLIDES NOW SUCH MATTERS REFLECT ETERNITY, FRAMED AS THEY ARE IN THE IMMORTAL REGIONS WHERE NEWCOMER AND COMMISERATING NO DOUBT ON THE ABSENCE OF WRITING MATERIALS IN THIS STATION BUT THAT WOULD BE TOO TEMPORAL A MATTER TO DWELL UPON, AND SO HE WAS THE RUBE. INDEED, THE ONLY ONE WHO CALLED ME THAT WAS MAURICE WHO HAD TAKEN A FONDNESS TO IT I DID NOT SHARE." (Letter to the author, November 2, 1990.)

HIGH REGARD & LOW ESTEEM

The persons Norman most admired and whose company he most enjoyed tended to be those (like himself, in fact) who possessed and passionately pursued an individual vision and were indifferent to peer and popular approval and commercial or critical success. (Fellow members of "The Lone Wolf Tribe," you might say.) I asked him in a letter whether during his time in Paris he had known Vali Myers. [Vali Myers 1930-2003, was an Australian artist and dancer who lived in extreme poverty on the left bank of Paris during the post-war years. See *Vali Myers: drawings 1949-1979* London: 1980 & *Vali Myers: A Memoir* by Gianni Menichetti, Fresno, Ca. 2006.] Norman replied quickly and eagerly to my inquiry, saying that having read my question concerning Vali, he had been inspired to "immediately jump to the typewriter impelled by the burst like just now coming upon your asking me if I knew Vali." "Yes, indeed I did," he wrote, "and it's just about the last one I'd have imagined you'd come up with. I was in Rome at the time, living at the American Academy. I have photos of her, a truly remarkable character, in many ways one of the truly genuine people I have ever met." (Letter to the author, December 7, 1988.)

In a subsequent letter, returning to the topic of Vali Myers, Norman recalled: "the hotel where she was staying, the one they claim was run by Proust's housekeeper ... I remember well as having two windows with the shades drawn. Vali propped up with a pad, drawing. Some years before she was a night owl, seen at various times at a distance. ... I ran into her in Rome and she didn't have a place to stay so she came with me to my place. ... It's true she spent an hour doing her eyes. It was the only thing she took such minute care of. That, and her drawing. There is no doubt whatsoever that she is unique. Mostly perhaps because she knows who and what she is and stays true to herself." (Letter to the author, January 25, 1989.)

Another figure who exemplified the heroic to Norman was his Greek friend, Minos, whom he knew in Paris and later met while visiting London and Copenhagen. [Minos Argyrakis, 1919-1998, painter, cartoonist, satirist & poet.] Norman admired Minos' total presence in the present moment, his absolute, passionate involvement in art or conversation, politics, philosophy, melancholy, laughter or love, his ferocious energy, his insatiable appetite for life. Norman recalled one emblematic moment when present at a sedate gathering, he witnessed Minos enter the room: "His entry was explosive. The room burst to life ... galvanized by this Greek's electric personality." (Letter to the author, April 18, 1990.)

In the realm of art, Norman regarded with particular disfavour what he called "professionalism," by which he meant careerism, the churning out of work that was trendy, formulaic, skilled but devoid of originality, honesty or vitality. (For Norman, the embodiment of this type of artist was Andy Warhol.) He referred to his own position in the art world as that of "ever-abiding amateurship." "What I mean by amateur," he continued, "is a sense of non-status, as opposed to professional as meant by whatever Wall Street means by it. Before this begins to sound like sour grapes I should point out that it is a state of mind, akin to a child's, a state too easily sacrificed for the schemes and cunning required for merely coping in this vale of commerce." (Letter to the author, May 9, 1989.) The particular sense in which Norman understands the term "amateur" is clearly related to that of its Latin root in the word *amare,* meaning to love, to be in love with, to take pleasure in.

Further to Norman's aversion to artistic fashions and vogues, trends and movements, see his trenchant satirical estimation of the art world in *The Boiler Maker* by Akbar del Piombo, Paris: The Olympia Press, New York: The Citadel Press, 1961.

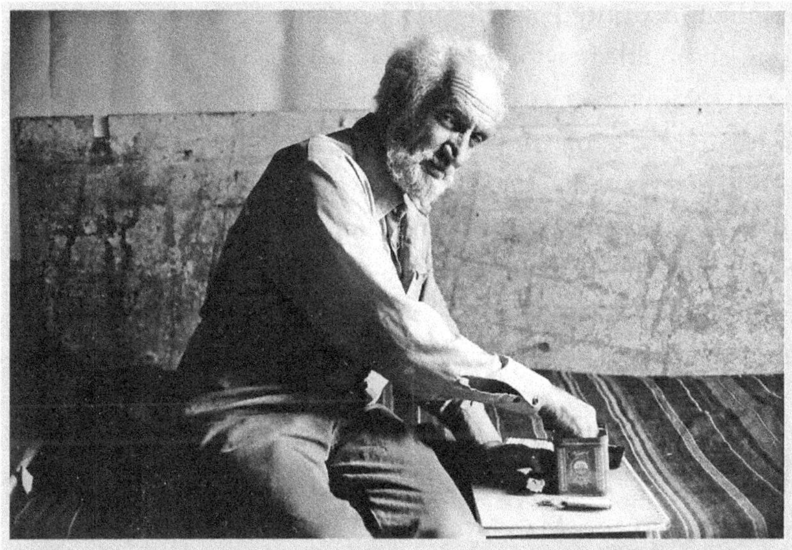

Photograph by Frank Monaco, courtesy of Earl Rubington

THE END AND AFTER

Norman Rubington died in the early hours of January 1, 1991. His brother, Earl Rubington wrote to me: "He had dinner at a friend's apartment on New Year's Eve. After midnight they went out to watch fireworks. On the street outside the apartment, he said he didn't feel so good. They returned to her apartment. She suggested that he go to the hospital; he didn't want to. He died in her apartment around 1:15 a.m. She had earlier called for an ambulance when she noted that his breathing became labored. When his breathing stopped, she tried CPR for twenty minutes but to no avail." (Letter to the author from Earl Rubington, January 26, 1991.)

A few incidental details: In an obituary of Norman Rubington printed in *The Independent,* London, January 10, 1991, the publisher John Calder notes that at the time of his death, Norman was calling on the widow of Maurice Girodias "with a bottle of rum to help her cold." Girodias' widow would be Dr. Lilla Cabot Lyon whom Girodias married on June 27, 1974, and from whom he later separated, returning to France. Norman's cousin and agent, Ann May Greene wrote to me that his last words were that "he hoped he lived long enough to go to the Academy," He was, she wrote, to have been the recipient of an award from the Academy of Arts and Letters, and such awards are not made posthumously. "It's like the final irony!" she added. (Letter to the author from Ann May Greene, March 11, 1991.)

In another, later letter, Earl Rubington wrote to me that he had made five trips back and forth from his home in Wellesley Hills, Massachusetts to Norman's Bleecker Street apartment, bringing back with him carloads of materials from his brother's many creative endeavors. "In the basement of our house," Earl Rubington wrote, "there are now more than

40 cartons, seven suitcases, and perhaps 10 attaché cases. These are filled with movies he made, clippings he cut out for collage novels, sketchbooks, collage novels in progress, journals and assorted memorabilia." In addition, "at least 120 paintings were shipped" to Ann May Greene, who had long been a faithful admirer and an active supporter of his art. (Letter to the author from Earl Rubington, March 21, 1991.)

The materials that Earl Rubington describes in the above letter were later donated by him to Yale University, where they are housed in the Beinecke Rare Book and Manuscript Library. "The Norman Rubington Papers," as the collection is designated, comprises writings, films and artwork. Unpublished writings held in the collection include two collage novels by Akbar del Piombo: *New York via Pluto* and *Proxy F.O.O.L.S*, as well as a book titled *Demi-Tasse, The Intimate Coffee Table Book: An Investigation into the Life & Times of Akbar del Piombo*. Additionally, there are typescript screenplays, short story collections, poetry, and numerous other prose manuscripts. (In the course of our correspondence, Norman sent me manuscripts of three unpublished collage novels: *Custom Made Déja Vu, The Use of the Phallus in Public Relations,* and *Being,* together with an illustrated story titled *Blue Food.*) It is devoutly to be hoped that all of these books will someday appear in print. Their publication but awaits the advent of some enterprising, neo-hip publisher.

Tireless in her promotion of her cousin's work, Ann May Greene has been a central figure in inspiring and generously assisting retrospectives of Norman's paintings. The first such retrospective exhibition of Norman Rubington's work, titled "Full Circle: New York, Paris, Rome, London, New York," was organized by Lisa Tremper Hanover, and hosted by the Berman Museum of Art from July to October of 2005. "An American in Paris: Norman Rubington's Mid-century Paintings" was on display at the Melvin Art Gallery in Florida, from March 5th to the 22nd in 2010. Another landmark retrospective was "From the Studio: the World of Norman Rubington," initiated and organized by Dr. Janine Utell and held at the Widener Art Gallery from August to October of 2015. More recently, "Norman Rubington: Retrospective of an Expatriate," an extensive presentation of the artist's paintings and graphic work, curated by Santa Bannon-Shillea of the Santa Bannon Fine Art Gallery, was held from September to May of 2016.

A 23 minute film, titled "Norman Rubington: A Documentary," chronicling the artist's life and presenting his work as a painter and writer, was produced to accompany the exhibition. The film is accessible on YouTube, see: https://www.youtube.com/watch?v=a4w35-g1of4&t=5s

Other figures significant in the fostering and furtherance of interest in Norman Rubington's art include Ilene Wood and Professor Abigail Susik.

Ars longa, vita brevis, as the old aphorism goes, timeworn, to be sure, but no less true for that. Norman is gone but his work has a life of its own. On canvas and on paper, paintings, etchings, the figures and colors and shapes so skilfully rendered by his hand, landscapes, cityscapes, portraits and still lifes – his lifework, the creations of his hours on earth, the expressions of his truest intentions – may still be seen and savored in museums and in galleries, as well as in images on the internet. Lamentably and unaccountably, at present, all of his collage novels are out-of-print, but are still to be found in libraries and in used book shops in many cities and countries and in various languages. *Fuzz Against Junk* is accessible at the online site of the *Evergreen Review:* https://evergreenreview.com/read/fuzz-against-junk/.

Vigorous and rich, alive with wit and bounce, imbued with sensuous attention and guileless amazement, worthy testament to an obstinate autonomy of spirit, his work survives him still and will, I think, endure.

CODA: GREGARIOUS ISOLATO

Norman Rubington was, by all accounts, (except, of course, that of Maurice Girodias) a generous, genial, gentle man with a gift for friendship, but in his allegiance to his vocation as an artist, he was uncompromising, intransigent and unwaveringly faithful to his own unique, oblique vision and individual version of things. After Norman's death, his friend Frank Monaco wrote to me that Norman "would not surrender to the market place as far as his work and belief went." Monaco went on to write: "he was for me about the most romantic OUTSIDER you could ever find in any society." (Letter to the author, May 8, 1991.) With respect to this recalcitrant trait, Norman remarked in a letter dated May 9, 1989: "I simply walk as an alien, for which I am well-suited from long experience." In his art and his thinking Norman never hunted with the pack, but remained from first to last a staunch and stalwart member of the Lone Wolf Tribe.

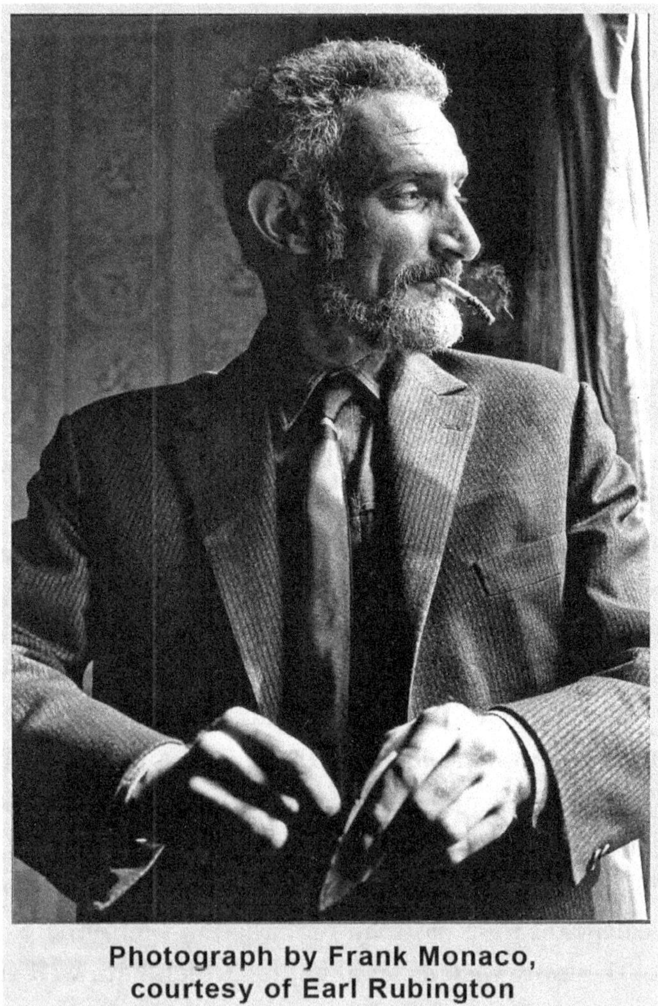

**Photograph by Frank Monaco,
courtesy of Earl Rubington**

9 788879 715699